D1383799

SIX WORDS
ABOUT WORK

from SMITH Magazine and MERCER
edited by Larry Smith

CONTENTS

FIRST EDITION

Designed by Nicole Salzano

Library of Congress Cataloging-in-Publication Data
is available upon request.

ISBN 978-0-9847350-0-6

Everyone has a story. What's yours?

SMITH

www.smithmag.net

Introduction SMITH

L egend has it that Hemingway was once challenged to compose a novel in six words. As the story goes, he wrote, "For sale: baby shoes, never worn."

The challenge is a provocative one. In 2006, SMITH Magazine, a website dedicated to personal storytelling, gave the form a new twist, challenging readers to write the story of their own lives in six words. We called the results Six-Word Memoirs. More than five years and half a million stories later, the Six-Word Memoir project has become a bestselling book series, a teaching tool and a powerful (and viral) way to express oneself.

People often ask what makes a good memoir. The answer is: passion. Each time we've launched a new six-word project, it's because we've suspected a topic would prompt passionate responses. When Mercer approached me about teaming up to examine work life in six words, I knew the topic would spark creativity and, yes, passion.

The short, short memoirs poured in from across the world. The project at smithmag.net/work offers thousands of ways to look at work life. This book represents just a fraction of them.

We divided the online project into four areas, reflected in the book's four sections: Why do you do what you do? What inspires your very best work? Best boss you've ever had? Biggest lesson you've learned at work?

Such sharing is a great way to get to the essence of our work life, and often the start of a longer conversation. When I called Debra Kirkley to tell her that her submission, "The five patients I'll always remember," was a prize winner, we talked a bit. I learned that she's a nurse in Seattle and that her short work story is about being inspired by those for whom she's cared: "I've practiced nursing for thirty years in five states. Every patient I've worked with has a story."

What is it about the desire to tell our stories? The book that started this all is called *Not Quite What I Was Planning: Six-Word Memoirs by Writers Famous & Obscure*. It contains nearly 1,000 stories. But there's one, by Nick Flynn, that I come back to a lot: "Many hands have kept me afloat." Nick's words are the perfect six-word sentiment for a project that is the work of so many people.

First and foremost, I want to thank the thousands who shared about their work life—good, brilliant, occasionally wild. Much appreciation goes out to our judges Gretchen Rubin, Anne Ruddy, Tony Schwartz and David Allen. Each is a master of his or her craft, inspiring so many people to work better, smarter and happier. SMITH associate editor Meredith Sires and designer Nicole Salzano are invaluable members of a small, hardworking team. Finally, thanks to Steven Faigen and the whole crew at Mercer for coming to SMITH with an inspired idea. They're pros—everything you want out of a partner and more.

With each story on SMITH Magazine our community becomes stronger and more interesting. I hope you'll share your story about work or any part of your life at smithmag.net.

Everyone has a story—what's yours?

Larry Smith, founder, SMITH Magazine
["Now I obsessively count the words."]

Introduction **MERCER**

People say fascinating things about work. That's why we approached SMITH Magazine about unleashing the collective power of the Six-Word Memoir community on this topic. The timing was right. Mercer had just finished updating its own employee research called *What's Working*™. We asked nearly 30,000 people in 17 geographic markets worldwide to give us their views about all aspects of work, including their jobs and employers.

This research helped us better understand what was on employees' minds—an important part of our work with clients. But we also wanted to capture the human dimensions of work: the very personal observations, experiences (both good and less good) and nuggets of wisdom about work that somehow apply to all of us.

So from June through August 2011, we teamed with SMITH to run a Six-Word Memoir competition about work—four separate contests, each on a different topic—that ran in the United States, the United Kingdom and Canada. The overall response greatly exceeded our expectations. We received nearly 8,000 submissions. They were by turns witty, uplifting, insightful, pragmatic and funny.

We have tried our best to capture those qualities in this collection. When you read through these memoirs, you can't help but gain a clear sense of the commitment and passion that people are capable of bringing to their jobs when given the opportunity to do so. And perhaps you will find within these pages a lesson or two that helps you navigate through your own workday.

Besides our entrants, a number of people helped make our competition a success. Thanks to Larry Smith and his team at SMITH for their guidance and flexibility. Thanks to our judges for making the tough decisions. And finally, thanks to the Mercer team—Ann Egan ("Marketing satisfies both left, right brains."), Brittany Daoust ("My Southern dialect often requires translator.") and Cynthia Chang ("Getting closer to the American dream.")— for doing great work and making work a pleasure.

Steven Faigen, partner, Mercer
["Thirty years working. Just getting started."]

MY JOB

Why I do what I do.

Dwelled on past, became an anthropologist.

– Jason Joyce

Writer, former engineer: I speak geek.

– Louise Julig

I nurse to repay
          past kindnesses.

– Franchesca Fenn

My charm only pays for
incidentals.

– Kierstin Bridger

Teaching's fringe benefit?
A literate society.

– Marlene Kimble

Certainty is overrated.
Became a freelancer.

– Jessica Berta

It's my happy place.
Most days.

– Doreen Price

Translator: Link between Canada's two solitudes.

– Paul Leroux

The corporate jungle
needs a Tarzan.

– Alicia King

I'm good at pushing around commas.

– Cheryl Della Pietra

Sought flexible conditions,
    became yoga instructor.

– Pamela McFarland Walsh

Philanthropist: putting money
where mouth is.

– Rob McKay

Little rocks can make big ripples.

– Jeanine Schill

By writing,
I create new worlds.

– *Marita C. Masuch*

To help heroes of small business.

– *Despina Panagakos Yeargin*

My brain understands
spreadsheets too well.

– *Kellie Freedom*

Middle school counselor.
Teenage angst specialist.

– *Carey Taylor*

Celebrating
birth to death
with flowers.

– Imelda Hinojosa

My words move things off shelves.

– Migs Marfori

`Selling vintage goodies:`
`Reaffirming recycling`
`matters!`

– Aimee Randall

Judging: not just my day job.

– Hon. Kristin Rosi

Who doesn't love
the payroll lady?

– Mindy Getch

**Aptitude for numbers,
passion for pensions.**

– Ian Weir

I feed the world.
I farm.

– Shawna Asendorf

Get a rush hiring great employees!

– Ann Belvin

**Technical jargon
eased for
mere mortals.**

– Nancy Chambers

When I'm playing piano,
hours disappear.

– Regina Masland

I'm making students
rethink their majors.

– Mary McConnell

I tell amazing stories in PowerPoint.

– Erik Weitzman

Amateur chocolatier...
making life little sweeter.

– Paola Iraggi

Would almost do this for free.

– Jean Feingold

Literacy lover
        brings stories
to children.

– Sarah Farbo

**Money and meaning,
        purpose and pause.**

– Patrick Matthews

People perform better knowing they matter.

– *Ellen Williams*

To prevent the
dreaded 3AM call.

– *Paul Nufer*

Because bacon won't bring itself home.

– *Garrett Jackson*

Satisfies my idiosyncrasy:
analytical
people person.

– *Cindy Upshaw*

Working to change
what "work" means.

– *Claire Elizabeth Terry*

Love helping people navigate real life.

– *Rita Welz*

The pay allows
me to play.

– *Ann Hodnefield*

Freelancer:
Always employee of the month.

– *Mary Elizabeth Williams*

This job?
Second choice.
First? Pirate.

– Elizabeth Kalman

I am Librarian, hear me whisper.

– Catherine Lee

```
My one-time fear turned
lifetime passion.
```

– Christie Beckwith

Because apparently
I enjoy herding kittens.

– Zack Soto

Personal finance expert: savings equals sanity.

– Jean Chatzky

After 38 years,
still not sure.

– Beverly V. Head

Social media specialist.
ADHD's new definition.

– Morgan Barnhart

**My clients'
lightbulb moments
illuminate me.**

– Fay Greenwood

I get to say kerfuffle.
Regularly.

– Susan Maloney

**Totem
pole
always
needs
low
man.**

– Steve Schohan

Finding right lawyers
saves their world.

– Melissa Denton

Had mid-life crisis, bought a bookstore.

– Praveen Madan

Freedom to challenge,
desire to inspire.

– Paul Reeves

**Making public workers'
golden years golden.**

– Lorrie Tingle

I promised ten-year-old me; I'm stubborn.

– Mariel Herbert

Work inspires me,
sharing
ignites me.

– Therrall J. Haygood

You cannot act
"on the side.**"**

– Kimberly Kelly

Helping patients die
comfortably comforts me.

– James P. Richardson

Because nouns and verbs rule universe.

– Evan Elliot

Help employees find
their way professionally.

– Kathleen Speer

No, seriously.
I teach laughter classes.

– Suzanne Pappas

**Great boss makes
it all worthwhile.**

– Fontaine Lam

Because brilliant ideas
die without encouragement.

– *Lucy Hawkins*

My classroom is my Carnegie Hall.

– *Lynn LeBlanc*

Patients need hope.
So do I.

– *Timothy Shea*

Dreams, duty,
and my little darlings.

– *Heather Dearly*

```
Hollywood
        has not yet
discovered me.
```

– Gina D. Curtis

**Bad at math,
        good with colors.**

– Jolie Foreman

Putting the "human"
    in human resources.

– Jack Kennedy

Possess a strange affinity for chalk.

– Lisa Bottone

So teens can make different choices.

– Hannah Kirby

People yelling,
        bosses hiding,
            I'm Superman!

– Richard M. Johnson

```
I love losing myself
solving problems.
```

– Vicki Gundrum

**Gives my other
        personality a home.**

– Coleen Goodson

Grandchildren need spoiling;
I keep toiling.

– *Kathy Johnson*

All employees benefit from benefits managers.

– Holly Hartley

Quietly telling my story through art.

– Anni Schwabe

```
You tell me;
I'm a researcher.
```

– Paul Harrington

That passport isn't gonna stamp itself!

–Davina van Buren

I get to calculate
people's raises.

– Geralyn Koehler

Leave a legacy I'm proud of.

– David Wright Walstrom

**Who doesn't want
to be awesome?**

– Kate Blaylock

My **super powers**
are needed here.

– Orchid Dobard

INSPIRATIONS

What inspires my very
best work.

Tell me I can't. I will.

– Geoff Saab

A need for "purfectshun"
inspires me.

– Dyan Titchnell

Student said I'm contagious.
Best compliment.

– Amapola Manuela

A secret passion
for flawless formatting.

– Joshua Hall

Helping others
when nobody else can.

– Robert Reeder

Difference to make,
legacy to leave.

– Arthur Chung

Freedom to fail.
Support to succeed.

– Beth Ferstl

If I'm breathing
then I'm writing.

–Rebecca Hosking

Thank you,
       well done,
good work.

– Mark Rosenblum

Caffeine,
    chocolate
and fear
    of failure.

– Brian J. Collins

I'm not the department director...yet.

– Jen Cadiz

An inbox teetering on
            imminent collapse.

– Kitty Maguire

Being someone
my child
can respect.

– Cathi Christina

Pats on the back work wonders.

– Jacqueline Rice

Down dog and "Om" between deadlines.

– Christine Hoehne

Every Monday
the horizon's the horizon.

– Russ Roberts

Can't quit.
I own the place.

– Cecile Moore

My gen gets no social security.

– Kellie Freedom

**Client said I helped her.
Success.**

– Josephine Collett

Hearing former
    students say thank you.

– Nicole Seiffert

**O p e n i n g books
to open closed minds.**

– Beverly V. Head

Neglected houses
    are my new canvas.

– Mary McConnell

To make life easier for others.

– Doreen Price

"You can't, you're way too old."

– Tony Reynolds

Boss saying,
    "Wow girl, you're good!"

– Carol Twyman

A future contributor
        to wider society.

– Samuel Dash

View from top
worth the climb.

– Donna L. Haring

I like proving
the naysayers wrong.

– Jo Myers McChesney

Housework. It cleans out my brain.

– Carol Patton

When
you are
against
the clock...

– Sue Hostig

Four words:
"You changed my life."

– Annie Farley

**Preventing being
voted off the "island!"**

– Jeff King

Newcomers are catching up.
Must improve.

– Lilla Gourley

Pleasing my inner critic.
Worth it.

– Heather Jones

The oft-missed beauty of the mundane.

– Amanda Green

**When they
are counting on me.**

– Bridget Gotz

Let's do it better with less.

– Victor Montori

Proving that words
can rewrite lives.

– Brittany Herman

Fighting for those without a voice.

– Beatrice Codianni

Attention to detail.
OCD a blessing?

– Nicole Brisker

**The five patients
I'll always remember.**

– Debra Kirkley

Helping retirees
live their best life.

– Shay Stephens

Receiving
brand-new,
shiny, and
positive
feedback.

– Alicia King

**Good idea,
enough time,
and persistence.**

– Cat Enos

Proving I will amount to something.

– Laurie Schmidt

Spiritual connection,
lyrical dissection.
Poetic possession.

– Tameka Mullins

Saving the world and cute shoes.

– Lizann Reitmeier

Helping
the little guy
get ahead.

– Jenny Foxe

Voices in head say, "Be better."

– Erin de Souza

Thinking
today will be the day.

– Wesley Coll


```
Bills.
    Deadlines.
Challenges.
        Retirement.
  Happy  hour.
```

– Beth Carter

Making my students laugh every day.

– *Trent M. Kays*

Someone saying,
"I need your help."

– *Wendy Brown*

The joy of helping
employees excel.

– *Heather Tuttle*

My puppy deserves
the best kibble.

– *Eugene Paulish*

A big idea, a hard deadline.

– David Boyer

**Appreciating me
   and validating
my contribution.**

– Roy Saunderson

Giving teens reason to geek out.

– Meredith Sires

Like hell I'm being
runner up.

– Zack Freedman

Full-time job with benefits and healthcare.

– Sally A. Lyons

**The bonus.
It's always the bonus.**

– Paul Beckman

A clear runway, a full tank.

– Steve Young

**Student joy after
challenging problem solved.**

– Jeff Raker

Impending
doom of
the missed
deadline.

– Lori Jones

The pleasure of sharpening colleagues' minds.

– Jim Gladstone

The customer whose frustration is eliminated.

– Steve Schohan

I thought I was useless.
Wrong.

– Cassidy Cameron

**Money,
money,
money,
money,
money,
money.**

– Milton Stephenson

**People understanding
my vision and dreams!**

– Lauren Tibbitts

**Pride in my hires
succeeding me.**

– Bill Thornton

The dawn's early light. Pure gold.

– Kay Reinhart

Lightbulbs pinging on
above kids' heads.

– Mary Jo Fesenmaier

Doing the right thing feels good.

– Alicia Salas

Everyone out there
who can't work.

– Hanna Barbaresi

**Across centuries, continents:
paying it forward.**

– Nandini Pandya

Trust me to do my job.

– John A. Law

**Proving some wrong,
   proving some right.**

– Kristin Overholt

Coworkers
who
thank me
years later.

– Michael Wenzler

**Watching students
find and use voice.**

– Lisa Bottone

An employer that respects
and rewards.

– Cindy Simbandi

Office artwork
from my two daughters.

– Fred Hibbs

**Change circumstances
by changing your attitude.**

– Maggie Alvarez

Watching patients
fight for their lives.

– Kara Carthel

Wanting versus having to do it.

– Kelly Heaney

Explaining
it all in six words.

– Tanja Cilia

**Tick
tick
tick
tick
tick
tick...**

– Siobhan O'Flynn

Parents sacrificed
so I could soar.

– Cindy Upshaw

Leave world better
than found it.

– Deborah A. Cunefare

**Respect,
trust
and
an
eleventh-hour
deadline.**

– Alexandra Benjamin

BOSSES

The best boss I ever had.

Asked for ideas, and used them.

– Deborah A. Cunefare

Said, "Conversations,
        not communications,
                drive change."

– Carolyn Burton

**Pointed out flaws,
sandwiched in praise.**

– Shauna Greene

Unconditional trust
        combined with
tireless support.

– Ben Jackson

Defined destination without dictating the map.

– *Laureatte Loy*

Two ears,
           one mouth,
engaged wisely.

– *Bob Myers*

Took responsibilities
     very seriously, not himself.

– *Anita Sanders*

Taught
me
to
think
for
myself.

– *Alicia King*

Made me look forward to work.

– *Kevin Kunreuther*

Lousy interview,
but you're hired anyway.

– Erin de Souza

Expected perfection, settled for my best.

– Kim Baas

Information flowed freely;
so did feedback.

– Jon Basden

**Provided guidance;
didn't take the credit.**

– Peter Ashkenaz

Was an enabler, not a disabler.

– Andrew Kehl

Allowed me to discover great talents.

– Dan Arrington

Motivated by ignoring my title's confines.

– Lisa Kucman

Saved my job time and again.

– Willona Sloan

**She guides,
I grow, who knew?**

– Eileen Weber

He said
thank you
every day.

– Robin Slick

The respect was earned,
never demanded.

– *Mark Rosenblum*

Hired renewable
resources,
not expendable
commodities.

– *Peri Mayes*

Played quarterback to my best touchdown.

– *Wesley Coll*

Fell from grace
defending his team.

– *Payton Kiser*

She stands between
us and trouble.

– *Kara Carthel*

Rolls up his sleeves, digs in.

– *Jeanette Cheezum*

Never drove a bus over me.

– *Jeff King*

**Helped me quit.
We're friends now.**

– *Charles London*

Never steered me wrong.
Trustworthy GPS.

– Donna L. Haring

First one in,
last one out.

– Rolando Ithier

Turned dissonant
workers into a symphony.

– Kitty Maguire

Laughed and sang across
the store.

– Kelsey McKechnie

Promoted truth,
      justice and,
eventually, me.

– George Sosa

Removed obstacles; was my lead blocker!

– Niki Ramirez

Kept his bad days
   to himself.

– Eugene Paulish

Knew her success
   depended on mine.

– Kim Forlizzi

She hired a formerly
incarcerated person.

— *Beatrice Codianni*

Prioritized
        finding solutions
over who's wrong.

— *Dickie Widjaja*

Knew my strengths, used them daily.

— *Jayne McManis*

Didn't pretend
        to understand;
trusted instead.

— *Zoe Price*

Rewards tenacity.
Respects veracity.
Recognizes capacity.

– Coleen Goodson

Encouraged us to fly the nest.

– Lisa Dickens

Advice:
"Don't fear future; shape it."

–Yusuf A. Shikari

Beer thirty every Friday. He bought.

– Lee Stoops

Wrote thank you on my paychecks.

– Michelle Peterson

**Understood laughter
was the best mentoring.**

– Terri Hoehne

Made the rounds
and chatted daily.

– Paul Leroux

**Always brought
us the good doughnuts!**

– Nadine Anglin

Two words:
        Not crazy.
HUGE plus.

– Sima Matthes

Listened, led, cared.
Every single day.

– Koeyli Jaluka

Taught me to navigate stormy seas.

– Karen Lewis

Discovered the strengths
        each employee possessed.

– Shelagh Delves-Broughton

Advised: Be CEO of

own workspace.

– Rose Atkinson

Dressed like Indiana Jones,
inspired excellence.

– *Katherine Larkin*

Left me hanging
out to try.

– *Diarmuid Timmons*

Cared more about employees than himself.

– *Kelly Heaney*

Fired me, said dreams need chasing.

– *Ronald Ray*

Gave me wings,
inspired great things.

– Aimee Bader

Threaded wisdom within
the day's minutiae.

– Victoria Bernal

Her hair was **big,**
heart **bigger.**

– Maryanne Stahl

Came as putty. Left as sculpture.

– Sarah Mathew

Evaluation conducted
over vodka on ice.

– Jacqueline Rice

**Not afraid
to get hands dirty.**

– Barbara Behan

My wife.
　She told me that.

– Chris Baker

Wait.
　People have good bosses?
Unfair.

– Lacy Foland

**Required excellence,
    encouraged innovation,
modeled integrity.**

– *Robin Adams*

The CEO knew every
            intern's name.

– *Elisa Shevitz*

**Challenges me, empowers me,
appreciates me.**

– *Sabra Sciolaro*

Knew the
    buck stopped with him.

– *Abigail Honeywell*

He hired me.
I married him.

– Helen Greggans

Said, "If he goes, I go."

– Jason Joyce

Never confused
a memo with reality.

– Keith Herrmann

Taught me how to write,
right.

– Maryanne Stahl

Hid tears behind a stern face.

– Matthew Knight

Stepped aside
          so I could shine.

– Mary McConnell

**Shame he couldn't have
        superhero's cape.**

– Dana Shaw

Encouraged me to outgrow my position.

– Stephanie Burke

**First,
second
and third chances!
Saint!**

– Jim Berman

Showed up.
    Stood up. For me.

– Delores Beier

Made me fight for first byline.

– Heather Maddan

Shouted
    "Get out now!" at 6pm.

–Atsuko Dudash

Mentored me and didn't mother me.

– Leigh Giza

**Memorized
        employees'
zodiac signs
        and Myers-Briggs.**

– Ashley Allen

Rewarded me with
praise and chocolate.

– Jenn Cowan

Worked with me not at me.

– Melesha Owen

Pointed the way,
　　watched my back.

– Andy Swantak

Corner office doubled as party space.

– Robert Smidd

Educates daily;
    demands return on investment.
                                – Karen Marler

`Talent's`
`like puzzle pieces;`
`everyone fits.`
                                – Johanna Swift

Wants me to win at life.
                                – Shannon Whissell

Just lets me do the work.
                                – Ian McLennan

LESSONS

Biggest lesson I learned
at work.

Always start with
assuming good intentions.

– Teri Edman

Don't hire geniuses,
       hire capable people.

– Larry Bradley

Persistence has more value than qualifications.

– Mitch Polack

Work like you
own the company.

– John Thornton

**Know security guards,
cleaners by name.**

– Wesley Coll

Need the facts?
Ask a secretary!

– Jim Berman

```
Never let 'em see you
Facebooking.
```

– Ashley Allen

**While cutting hair,
never say "Oops."**

– Molly Moblo Perusse

Underpromise and
        overdeliver to
avoid surprises.

– Lisa McVay

Laughter is the
best engagement tool.

– Kristen Strobel

Respectful to all big and small.

– Dorothy Barr

You're not learning if you're comfortable.

– Debbie Beets

Press
every
button
until
printer
works.

– Melesha Owen

Best work ethic is working ethically.

– *Mark Rosenblum*

Busy does
  not necessarily mean
productive.

– *Greg Conway*

Lose your temper,
    lose your case.

– *Sherry Beer*

It's hard to cross burned bridges.

– *Robert Reeder*

Don't whine.
Do something about it.

– Lyn Bulman

He who is loudest,
isn't "right-est."

– JJ Jay

No cutoff shorts on
casual Friday.

– Scott J. Wilson

Some things are best left unsaid.

– Howard Hulme

The "save" button is your friend.

– Gillian Ramos

Read every e-mail carefully.
Words matter.

– Lisa Qiu

Think twice
before you hit send.

– David Hayase

Always beware
of the reply-all button.

– Brian Sting

Teamwork
always brings out the best.

– Jonathan Clayton

**Don't worry
who gets the credit.**

– Keith Jackson

Do one more thing than requested.

– Gary Belsky

Never forget.
You can
be replaced.

– Dustin Weeks

Always make the boss look smart.

– John Beardsley

Don't laugh
while boss is ranting.

– Leslie Wolf Branscomb

**Screw-ups will happen.
Just own them.**

– Kara Carthel

Be a leader, not a boss.

– Barbara Behan

Cutting corners
        only creates
more paperwork.

– *Dyan Titchnell*

Treat each day
        like it's payday.

– *Jean Chow*

Sign the card. Eat the cake.

– Kevin Kunreuther

Only hire someone
         you'd lunch with.

– Amy Friedman

No task is ever too small.

– Eric Myszka

Always look behind you
when gossiping.

– Judy Amsterdam

**Cubicles
are
neither
private
nor
soundproof.**

– Leigh Giza

Walk the hall rather than call.

– Juliette Mirsepasy

**Job interviews
are great learning places.**

– Steve Schohan

```
Seek a mentor,
then listen closely.
```

– Larry Smith

Always bring an
extra laptop charger.

– Maya McNeal

**Never play
Don Quixote
against
management.**

– Patrick Dentinger

Own your choices
and their consequences.

– Mary Carvour

Being right isn't
always the point.

– Debra Kirkley

Almost everything is better with snacks.

– Cindy Chrispell

Skipping lunch only makes
you hungry.

– Linda M. Rhinehart Neas

If you don't know, say it.

– B. Saville

Speak up.
        Followers
fade into background.

– Andrea Clayton

**Surprise your spouse,
        not your boss.**

– Laureatte Loy

**People-pleasers
do not good leaders make.**

– *Nicola Behrman*

`Money is not the only reward.`

– *David Hayase*

**Add value —
otherwise you're a commodity.**

– *Randall Lane*

Give your heart,
keep your soul.

– *Heather Opseth*

Anyone riding
elevator, possibly
future boss.

– *Susanne Namdar*

Everyone loves you
      when you're billable.

– *George Sosa*

Free speech can be dangerous sometimes.

– *Kathy Helgesen*

**Someone at work
      reads your blog.**

– *Amanda Green*

**Job description
seldom portrays job accurately.**

– Teri Porter

Nobody died,
        it's not an
emergency.

– Lynnette Spurrier

Do not ever threaten to quit.

– Pat Grube

Follow your heart,
        not the salary.

– Kelly Heaney

Work ethic, not GPA,
    determines success.

– Belinda Hernandez

Get the hardest part done first.

– Cathy Smith

Whiners never win;
winners never whine.

– Maria Ayoob

**Conquered mountains
are above the fog.**

– Charles Murray

Supply your own
compass and rudder.

– Kitty Maguire

Bake the IT folks a pie.

– Molly Norton

Learn the
    ropes before
challenging
    customs.

– Pam Grater

Pretend impossibilities are possible.
They are.

– Sandi Hemmerlein

Never say never.
Never say never.

– Kim Parker

Like Boy Scouts say:
Be prepared.

– Jim Byrne

The small favors
always get remembered.

– Jennifer Rheingold

**Corporate outings:
Dress conservatively,
leave early!**

– Ted Balph

`Avoid all paintball
team-building games.`

– Mary Gordon

Always say please
and thank you.

– Lisa Wiebenga

Go outside the building to scream.

– Carol Wilson

Fail fast.
Learn fast.
Improve fast.

– Steven Robins

Bring a problem. Bring a resolution.

– Donna Hamilton

Everyone notices
when trust is absent.

– Yvette Taylor Rosales

It's simple.
Love what you do.

– Bryony Punt

About **MERCER**

Mercer is a global leader in human resource consulting, outsourcing and investment services. Mercer works with clients to solve their most complex benefit and human capital issues by designing, implementing and administering health, retirement and other benefit programs. Mercer's investment services include investment consulting, implemented consulting and multi-manager investment management. Mercer's 20,000 employees are based in more than 40 countries. The company is a wholly owned subsidiary of Marsh & McLennan Companies, Inc., which lists its stock (ticker symbol: MMC) on the New York and Chicago stock exchanges. For more information, visit **www.mercer.com**.

About **SMITH Magazine**

Founded in January 2006 by Larry Smith, with the tagline, "Everyone has a story. What's yours?" SMITH Magazine has become a leader in personal storytelling. SMITH is home of the Six-Word Memoir® project, now a bestselling book series, calendar, board game, live event series and global phenomenon. For more information, visit **www.smithmag.net**.

SMITH Magazine founder Larry Smith has spoken on the power of storytelling and how to engage a community at PopTech, SXSW Interactive, AARP'S 50+ convention and elsewhere. He's spoken and led team-building sessions at companies such as ESPN, Dell, Morgan Stanley, Google and Shutterfly, as well as at foundations, nonprofits and schools across the country.

One life. Six words. What's yours?

Since the Six-Word Memoir® made its debut in 2006, more than half a million short life stories have been shared on the storytelling community SMITH Magazine. In classrooms and boardrooms, churches and synagogues, veterans' groups and across the dinner table, Six-Word Memoirs have become a powerful tool to catalyze conversation, spark imagination or simply break the ice.

Share a Six-Word Memoir on work or any part of your life at **www.sixwordmemoirs.com**

Praise for SMITH Magazine's Six-Word Memoir book series:

"Let's dub this American haiku. You can read pieces in seconds or ponder the book for hours."

— *St. Louis Post-Dispatch*

"Six words are worth 1,000 pictures. All told, they made me Twitter."

— *Philadelphia Inquirer*

"Will thrill minimalists and inspire maximalists."

— *Vanity Fair*

"A perfect distraction and inspiration, and a collection that begs to be shared."

— *Denver Post*

Praise for the Six Words About Work challenge from SMITH Magazine & Mercer:

"A fun, creative challenge— a diversion from the doom and gloom."

— *The New York Times*

"Funny—and surprisingly sweet."

— *The National Post [Canada]*

"Six little words are oddly deep."

— *The Financial Times [London]*